Spain
Coloring The World

Anthony Hutzler

Sketch Coloring Book

Copyright: Published in the United States by Anthony Hutzler
Published July 2016

All rights reserved. No part of this publication may be reproduced, stored in retrieval system, copied in any form or by any means, electronic, mechanical, photocopying, recording or otherwise transmitted without written permission from the publisher. Please do not participate in or encourage piracy of this material in any way. You must not circulate this book in any format. Anthony Hutzler does not control or direct users' actions and is not responsible for the information or content shared, harm and/or actions of the book readers.

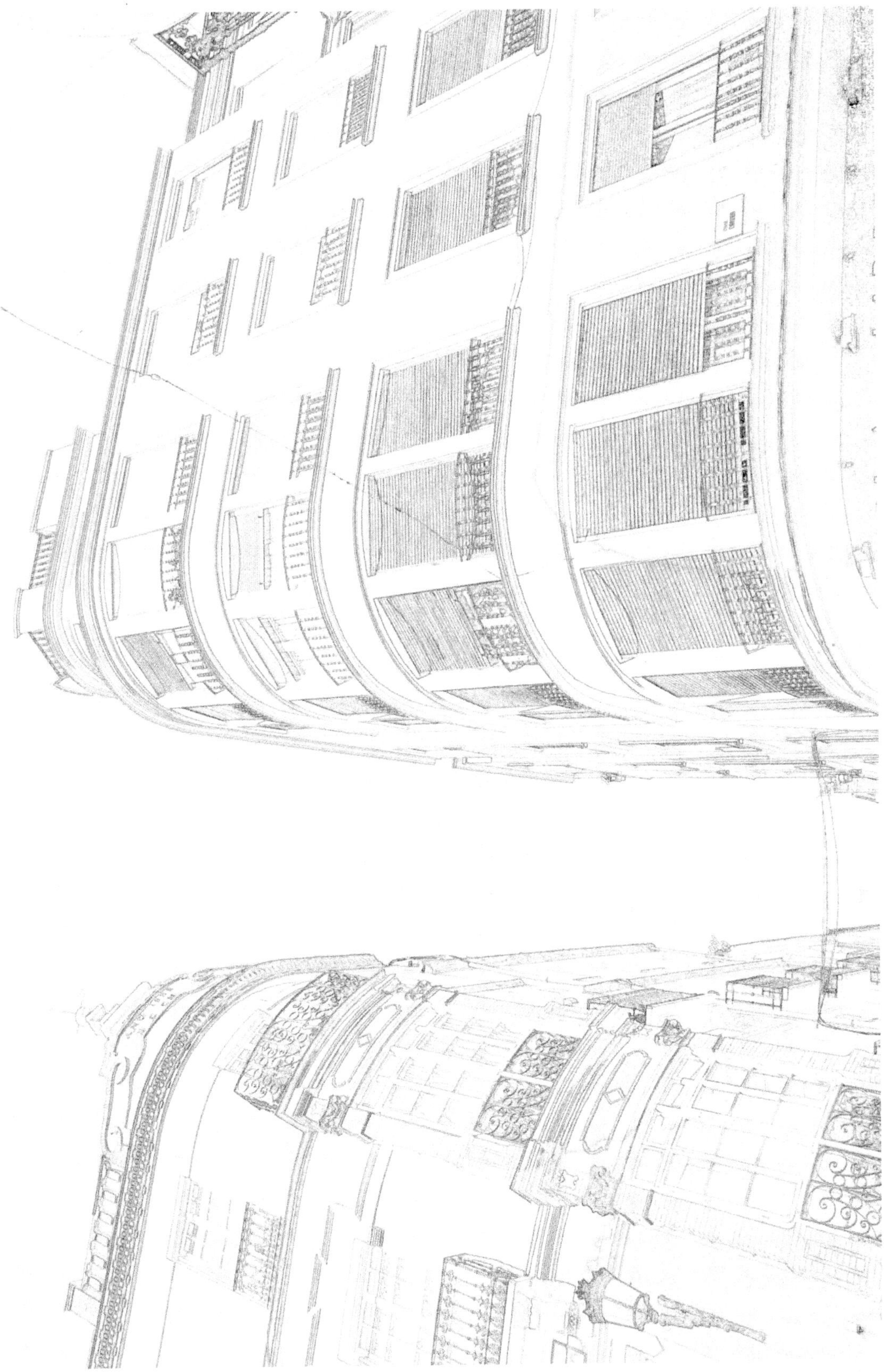

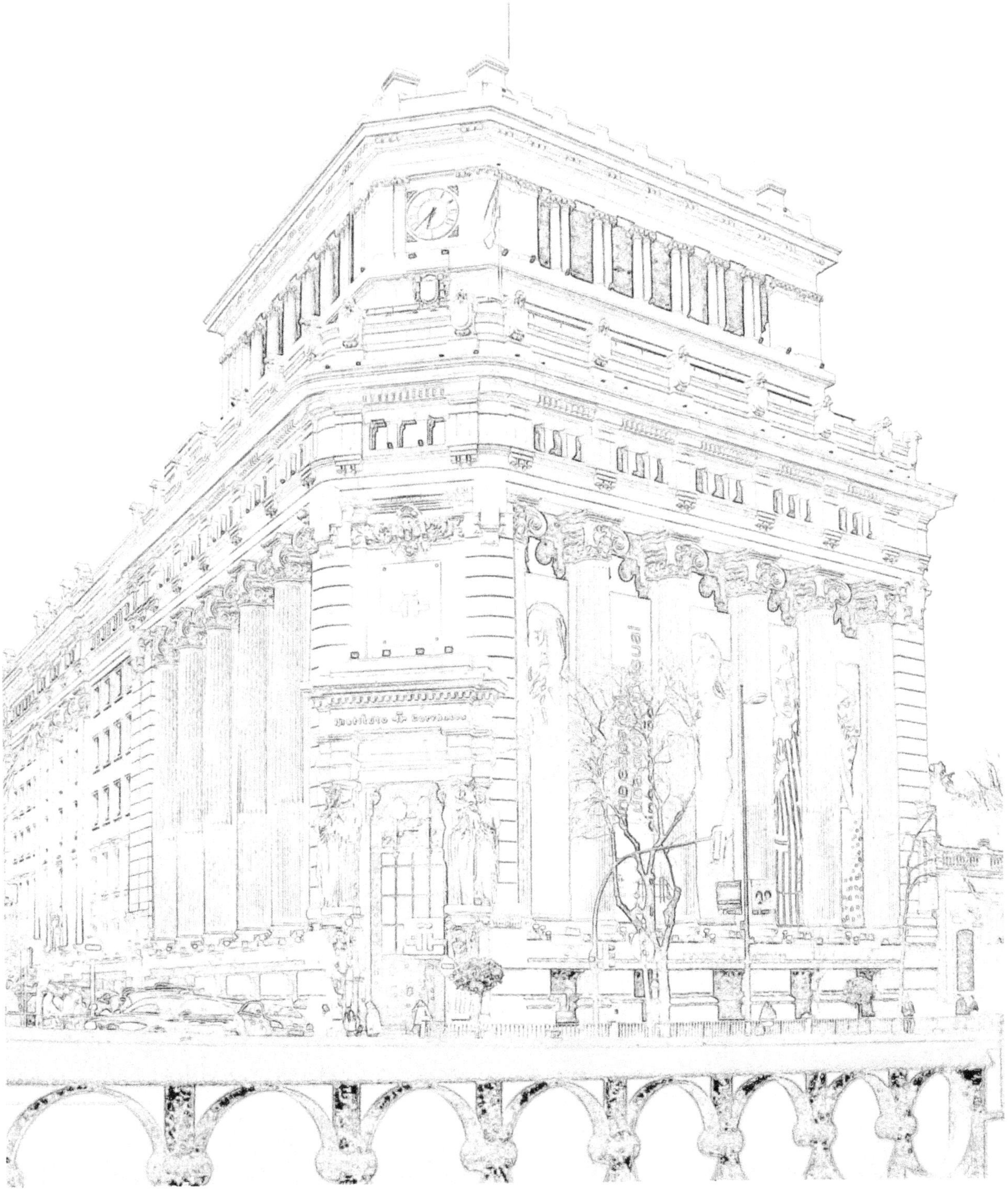

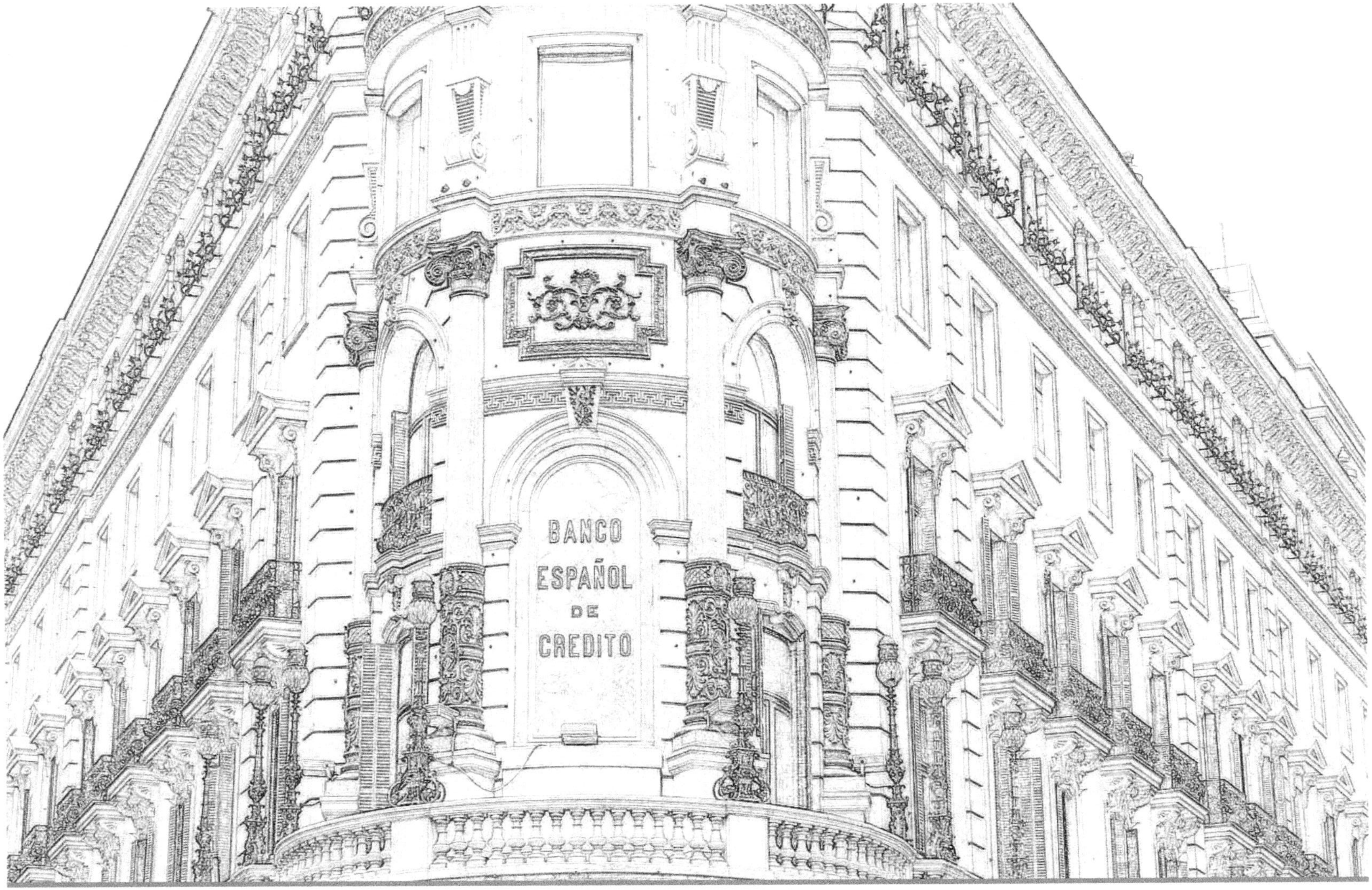
BANCO
ESPAÑOL
DE
CREDITO

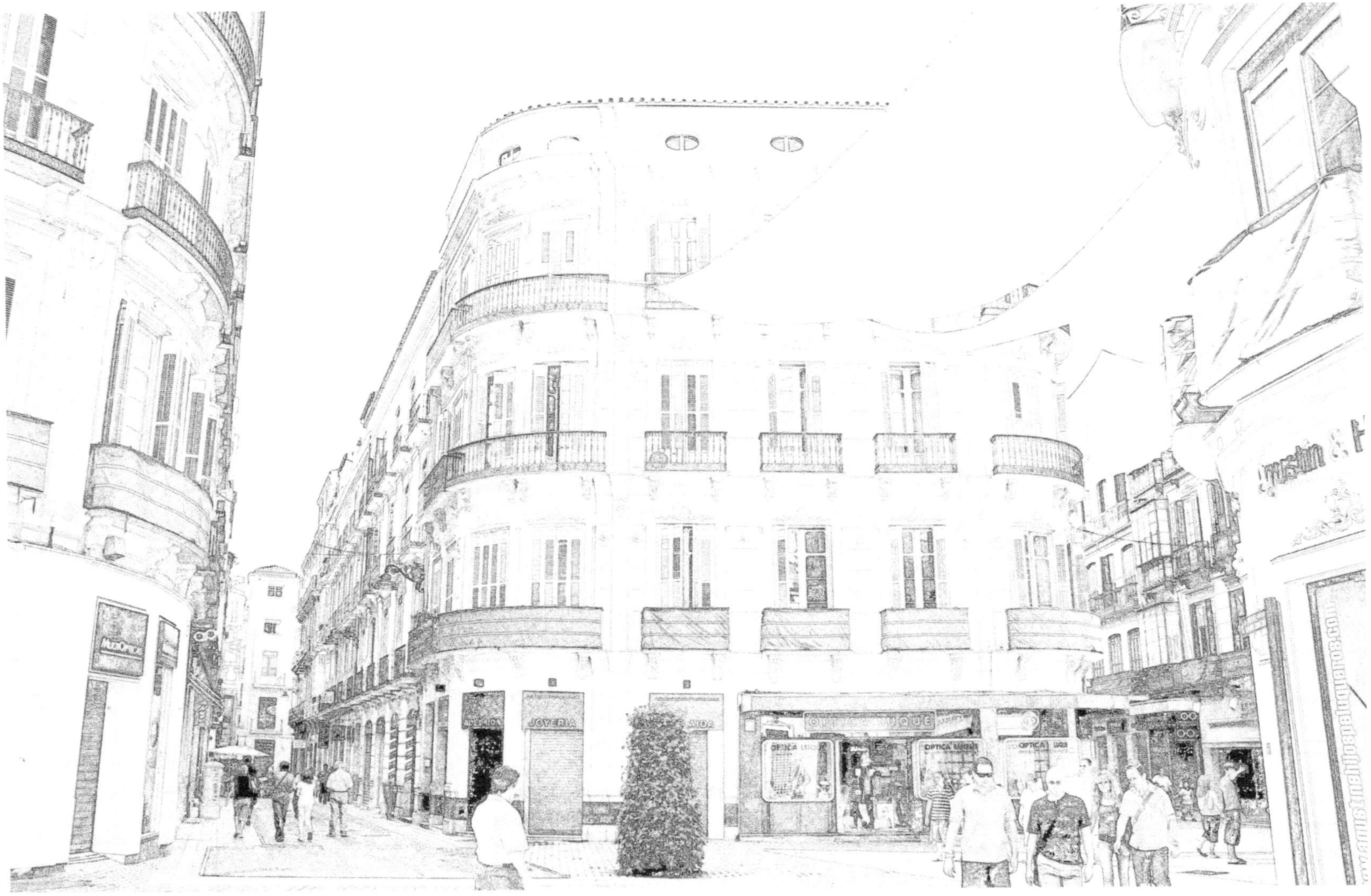
JOYERIA
OPTICA LUQUE

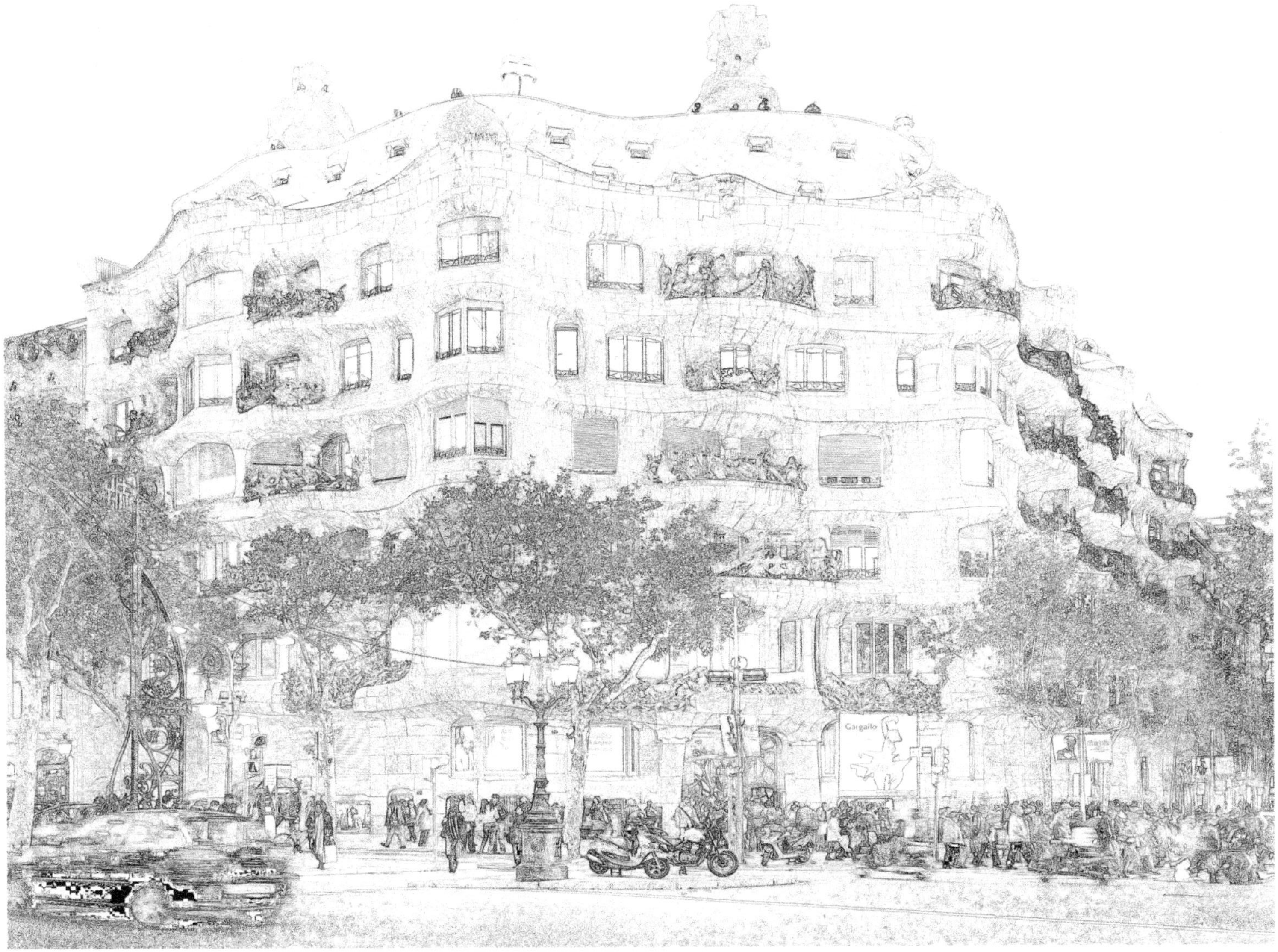
Gargallo

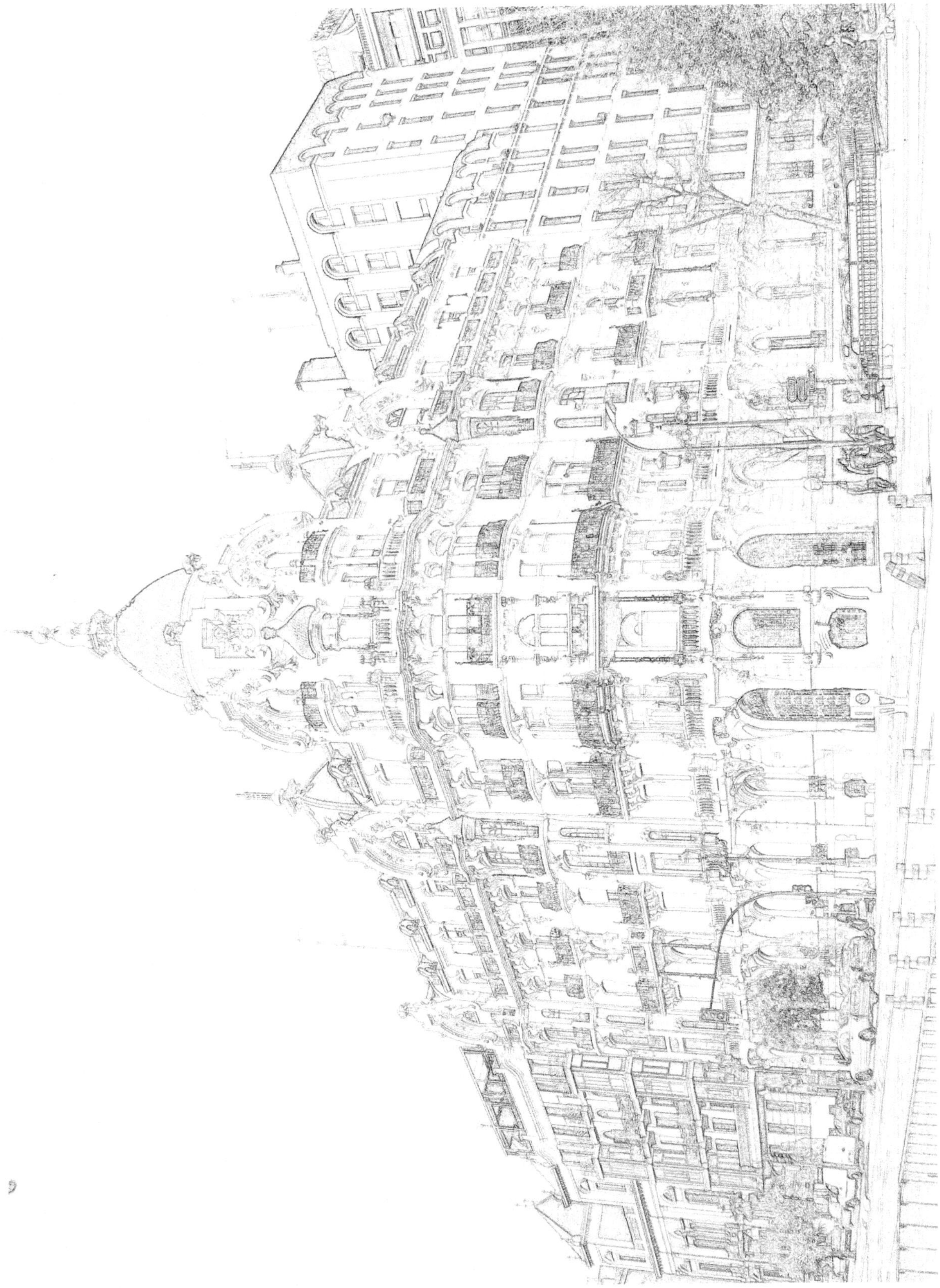

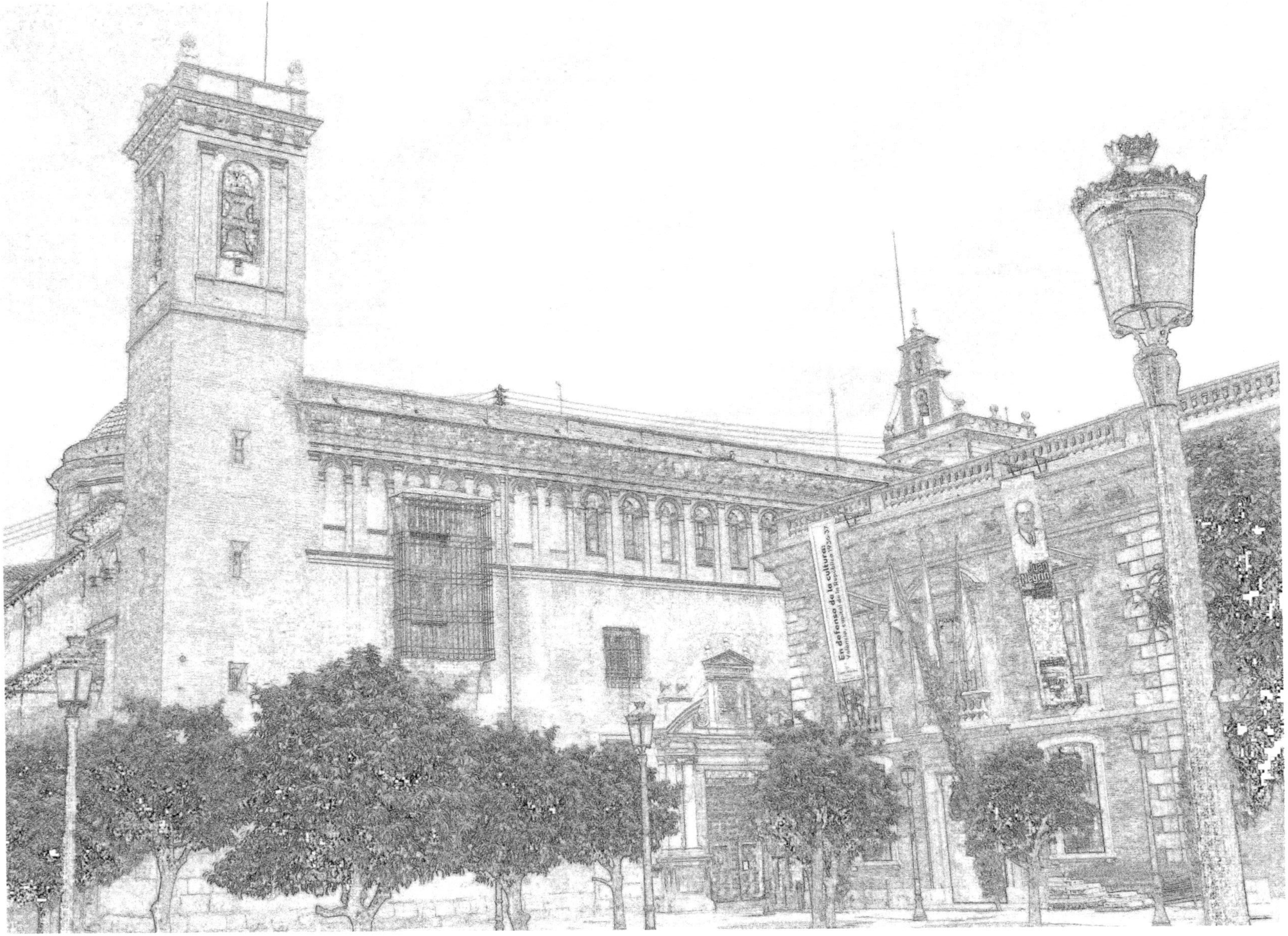

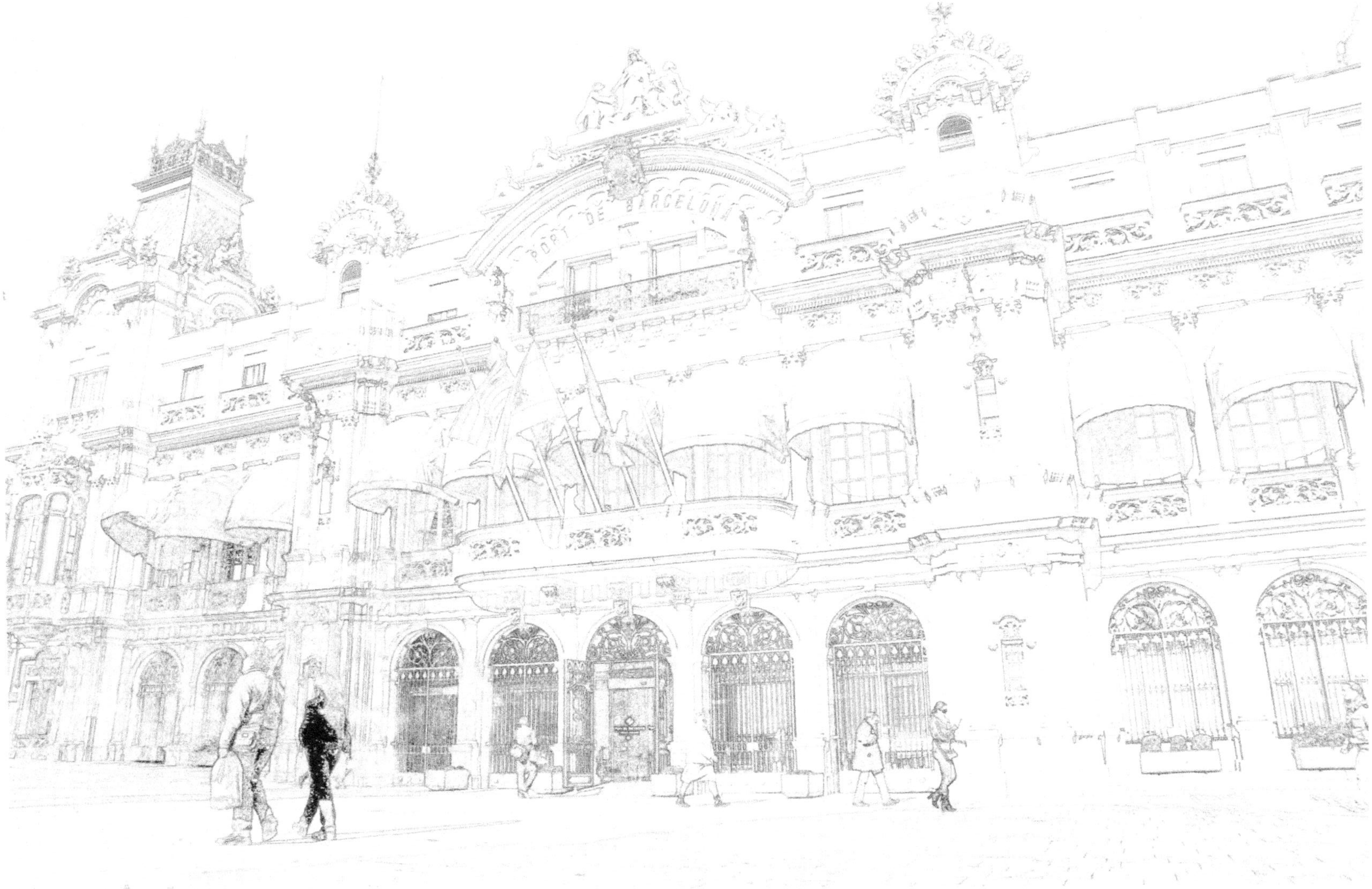
PORT DE BARCELONA

METROPOLIS

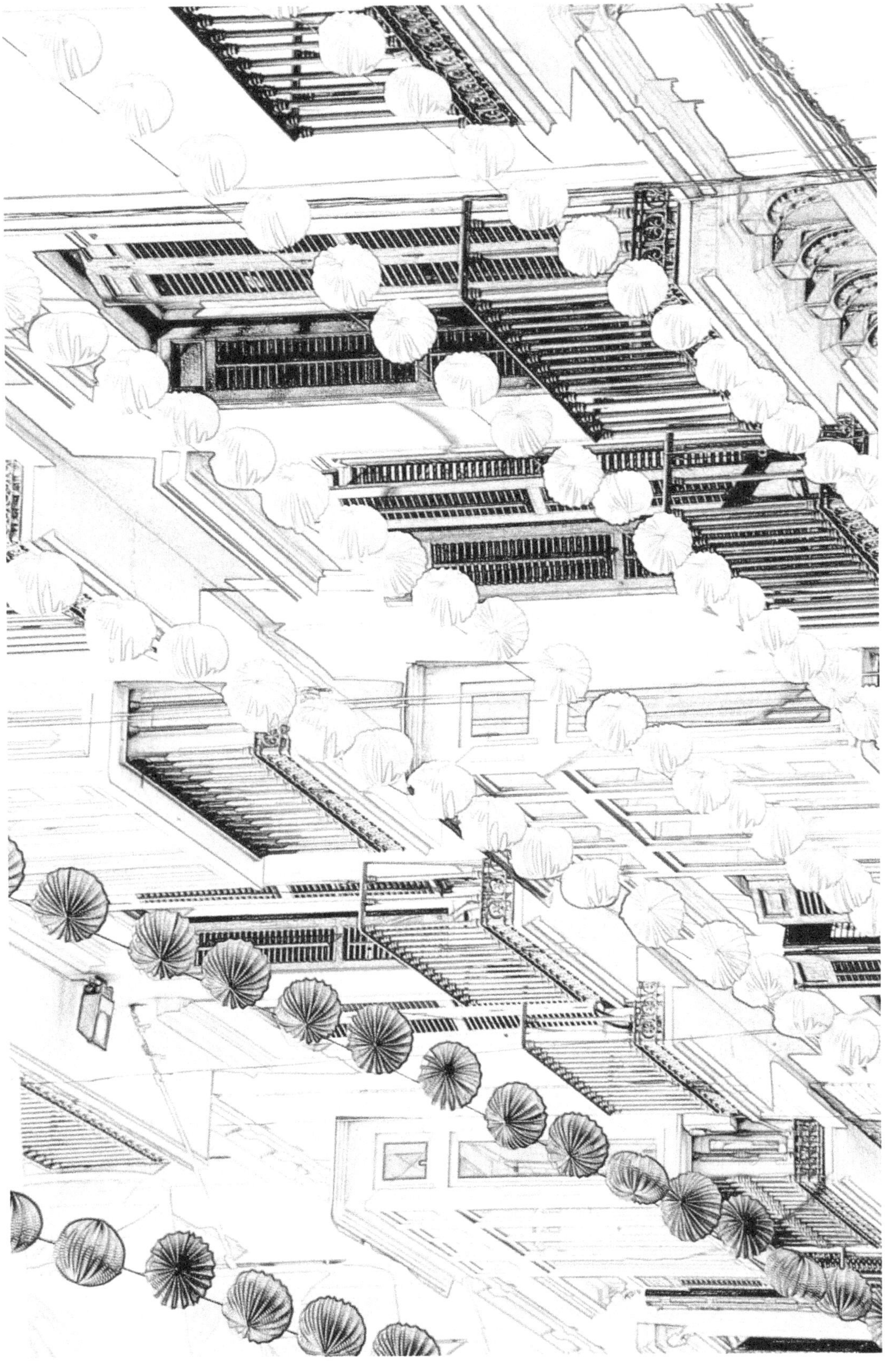

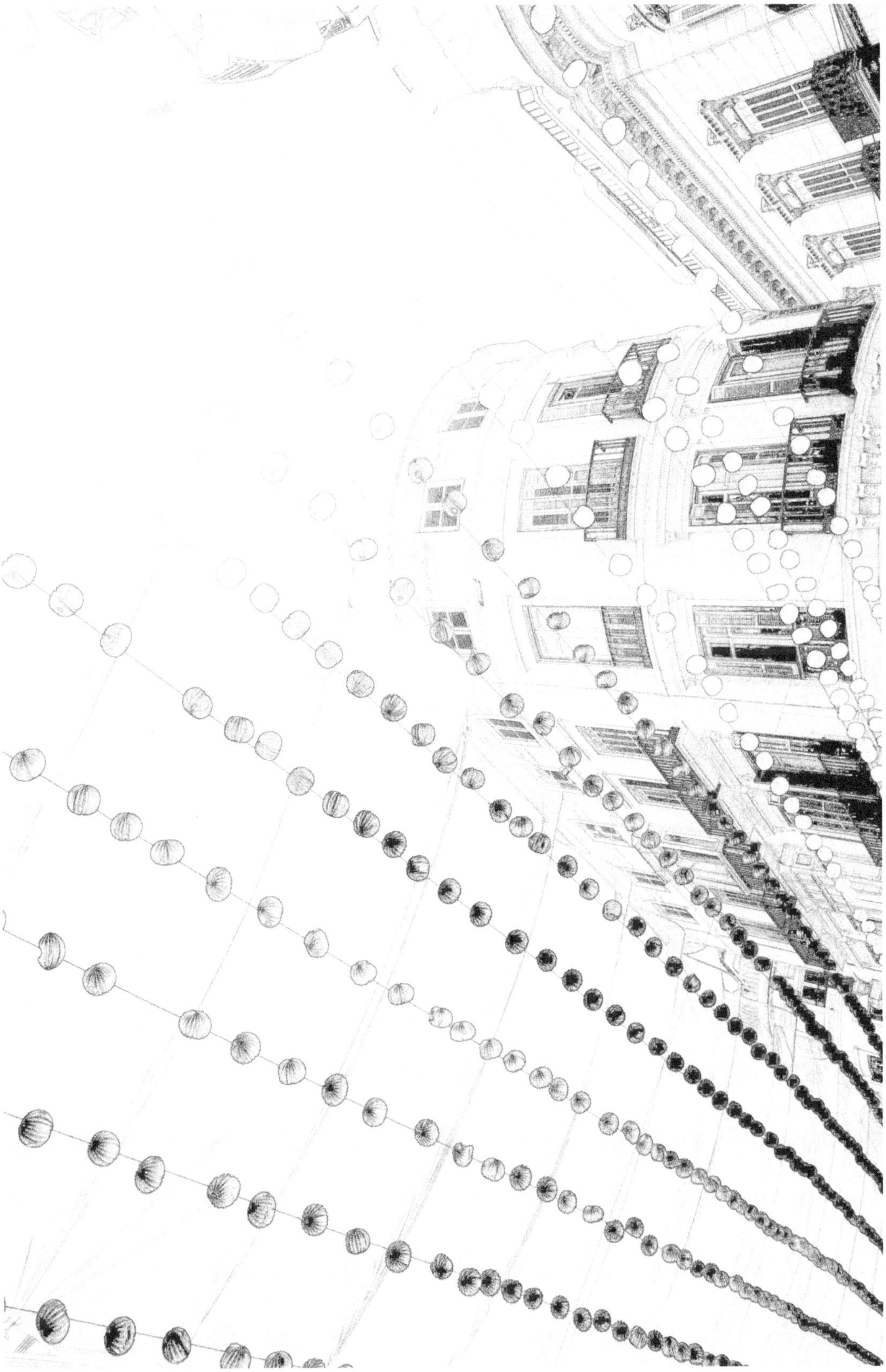

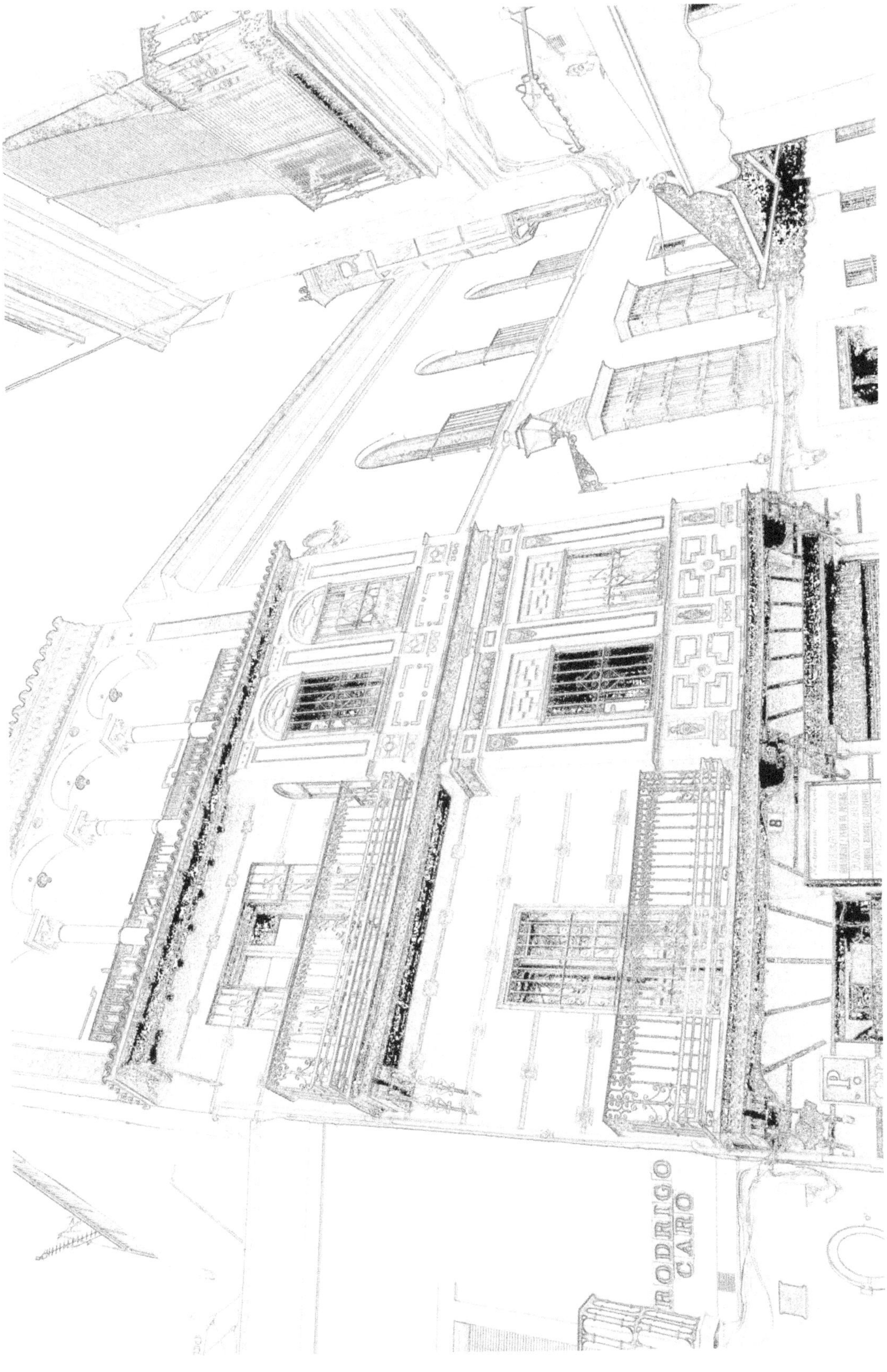
RODRIGO
CARO

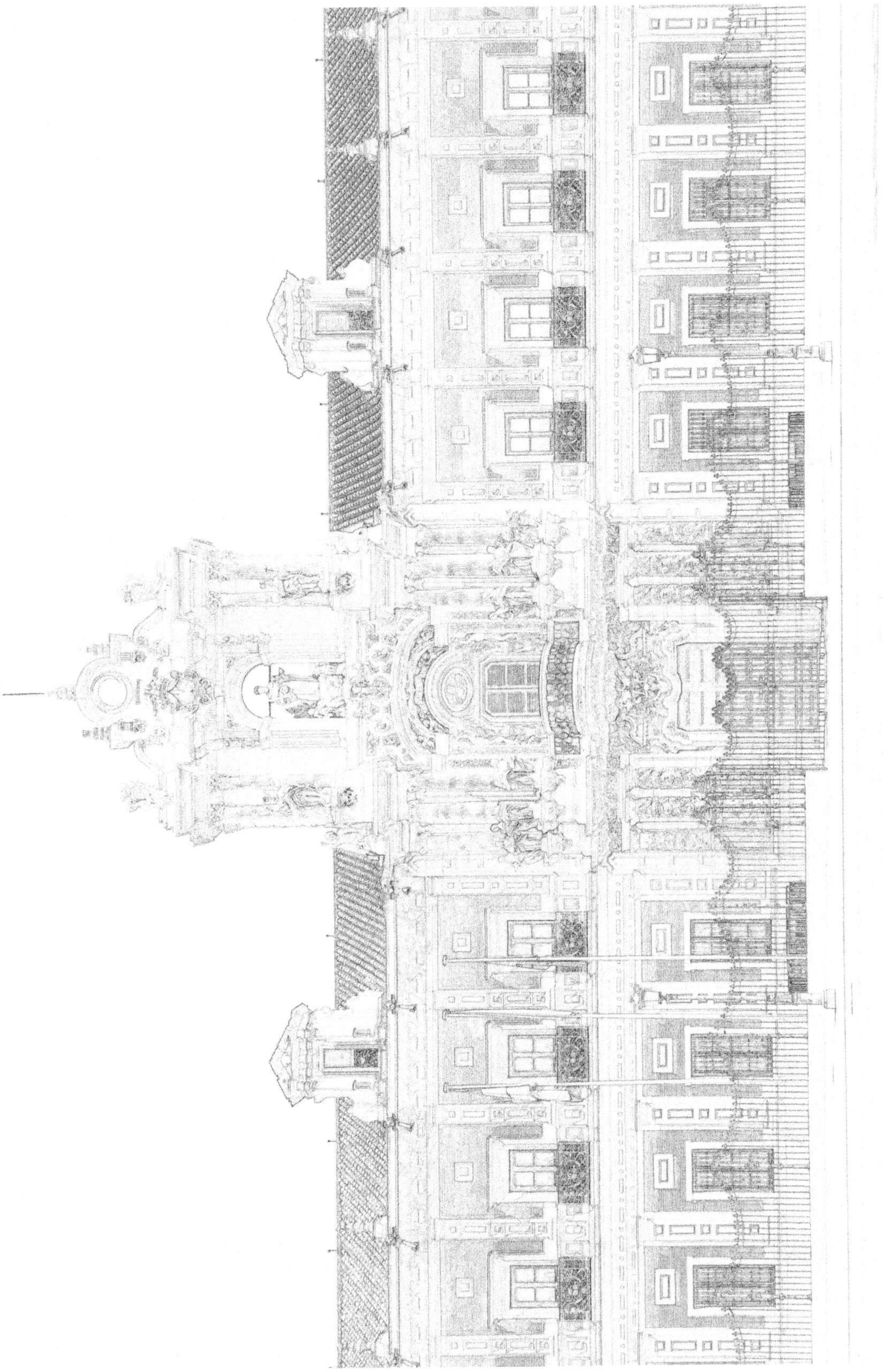

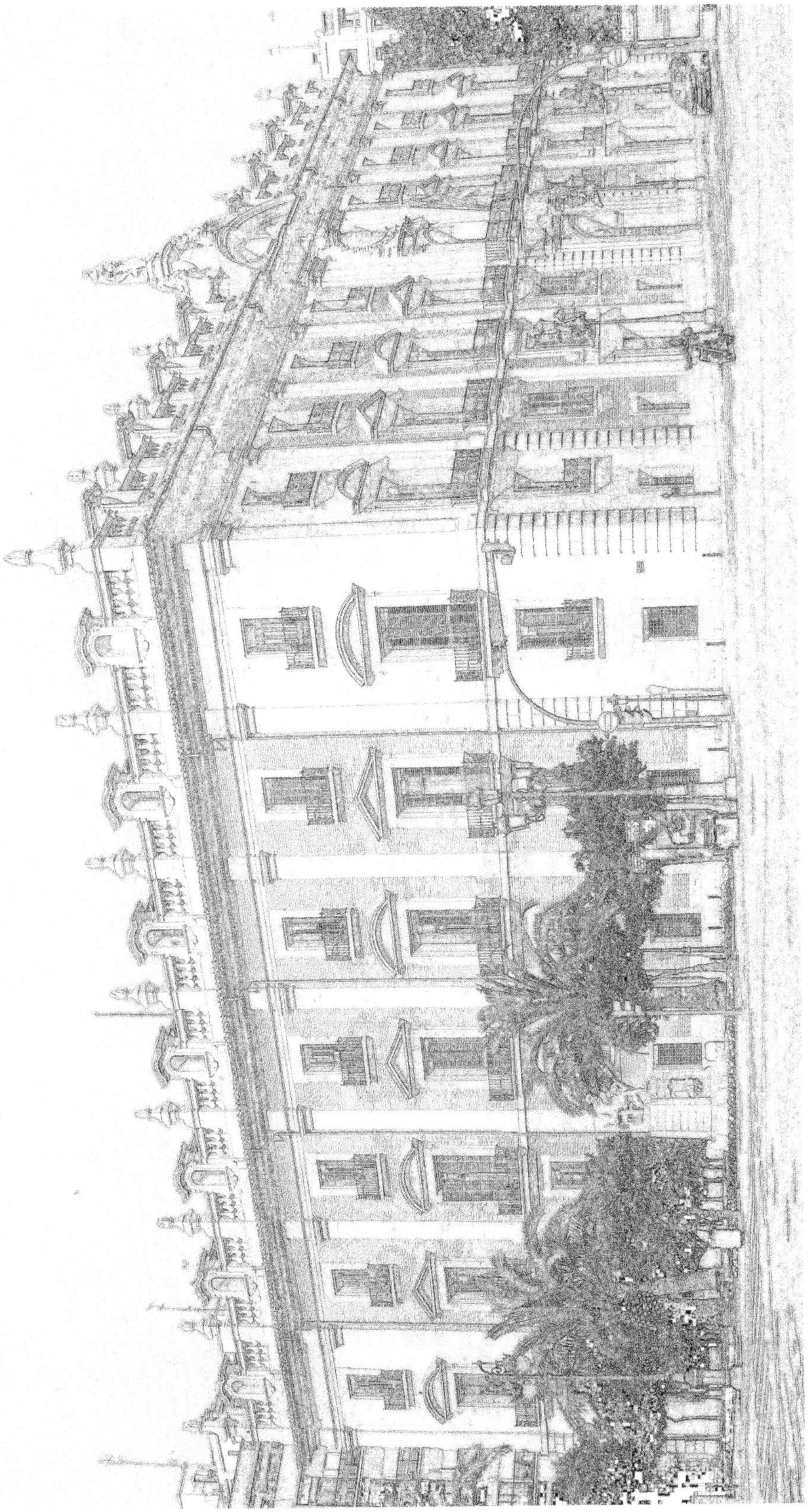

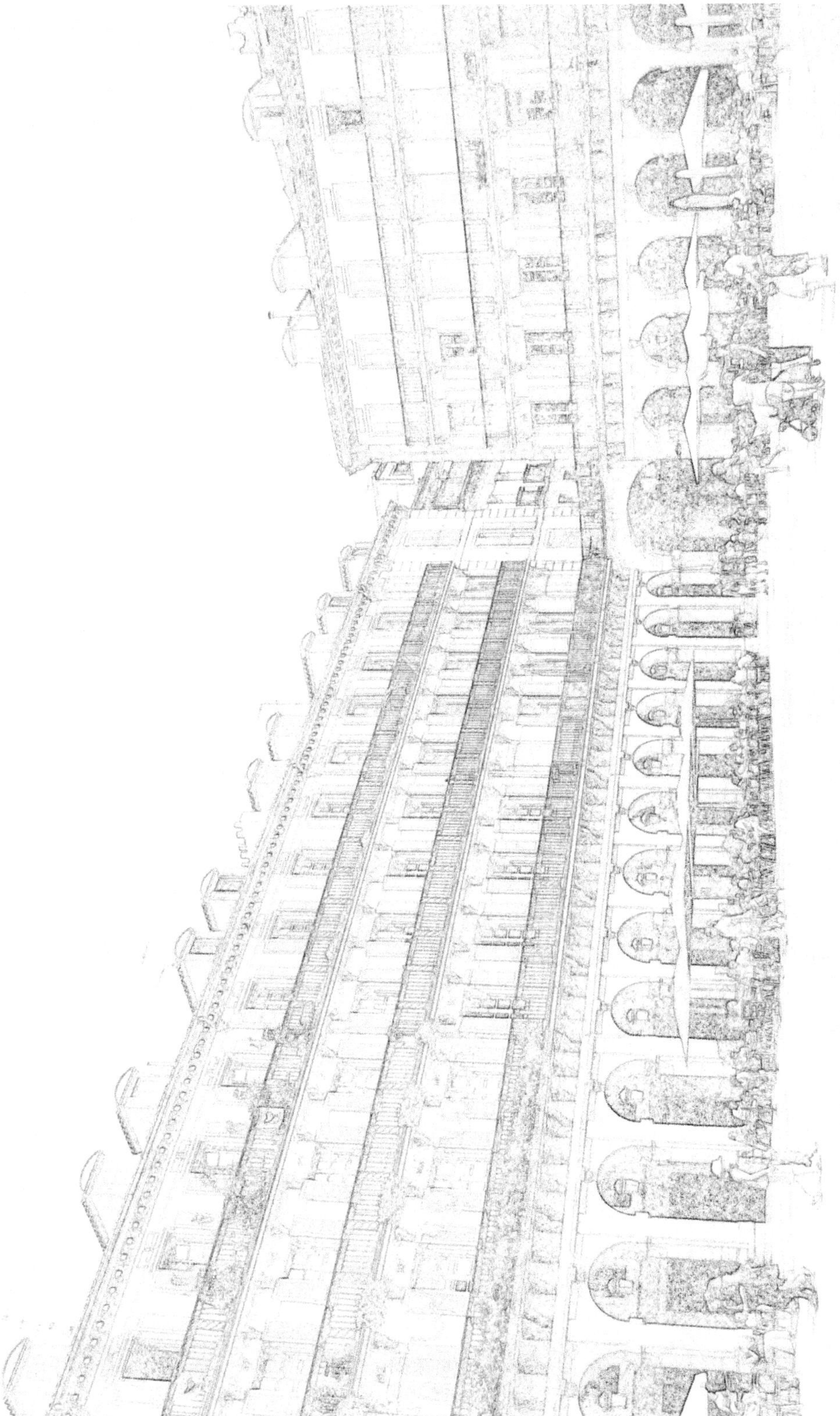

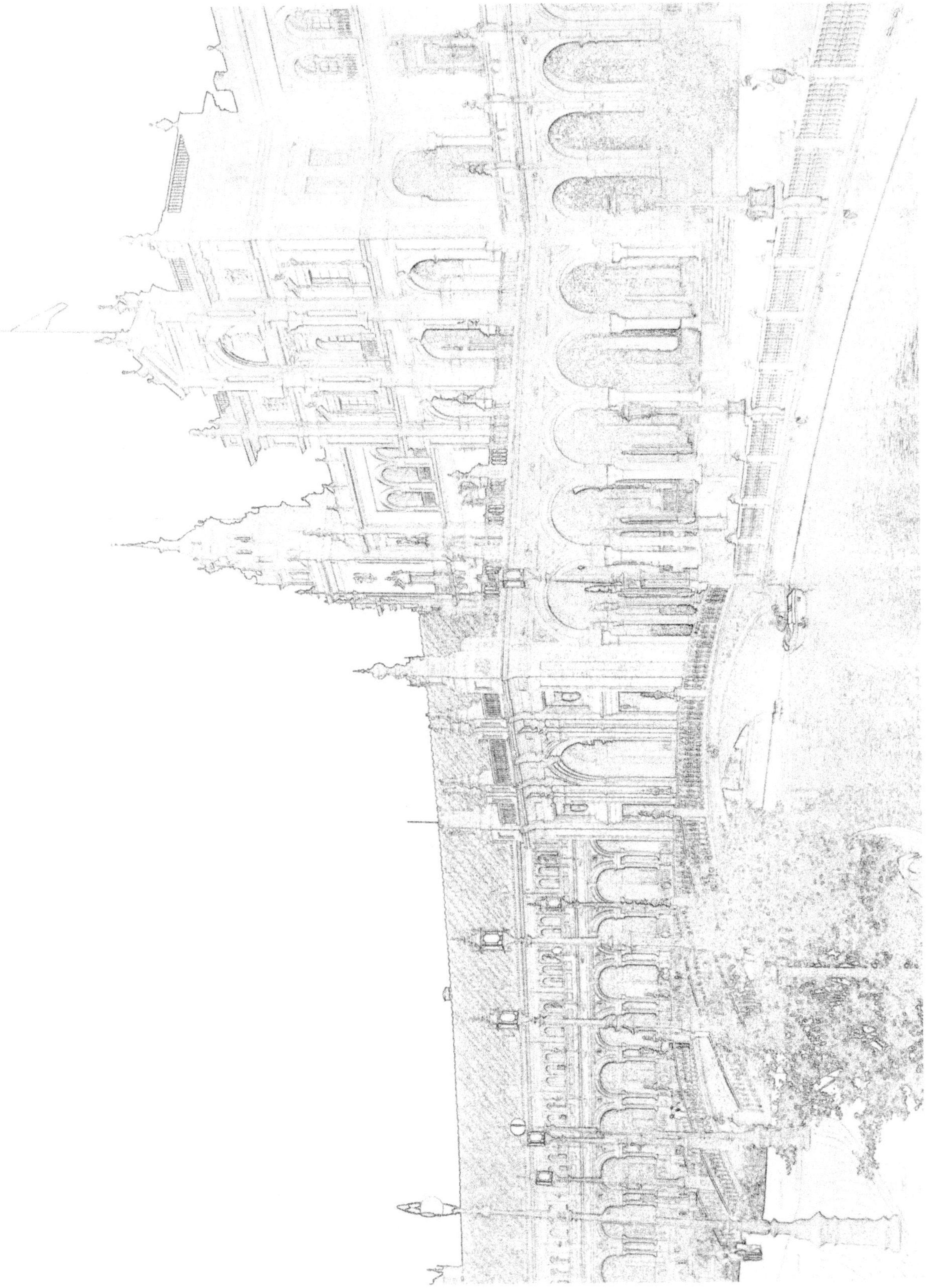

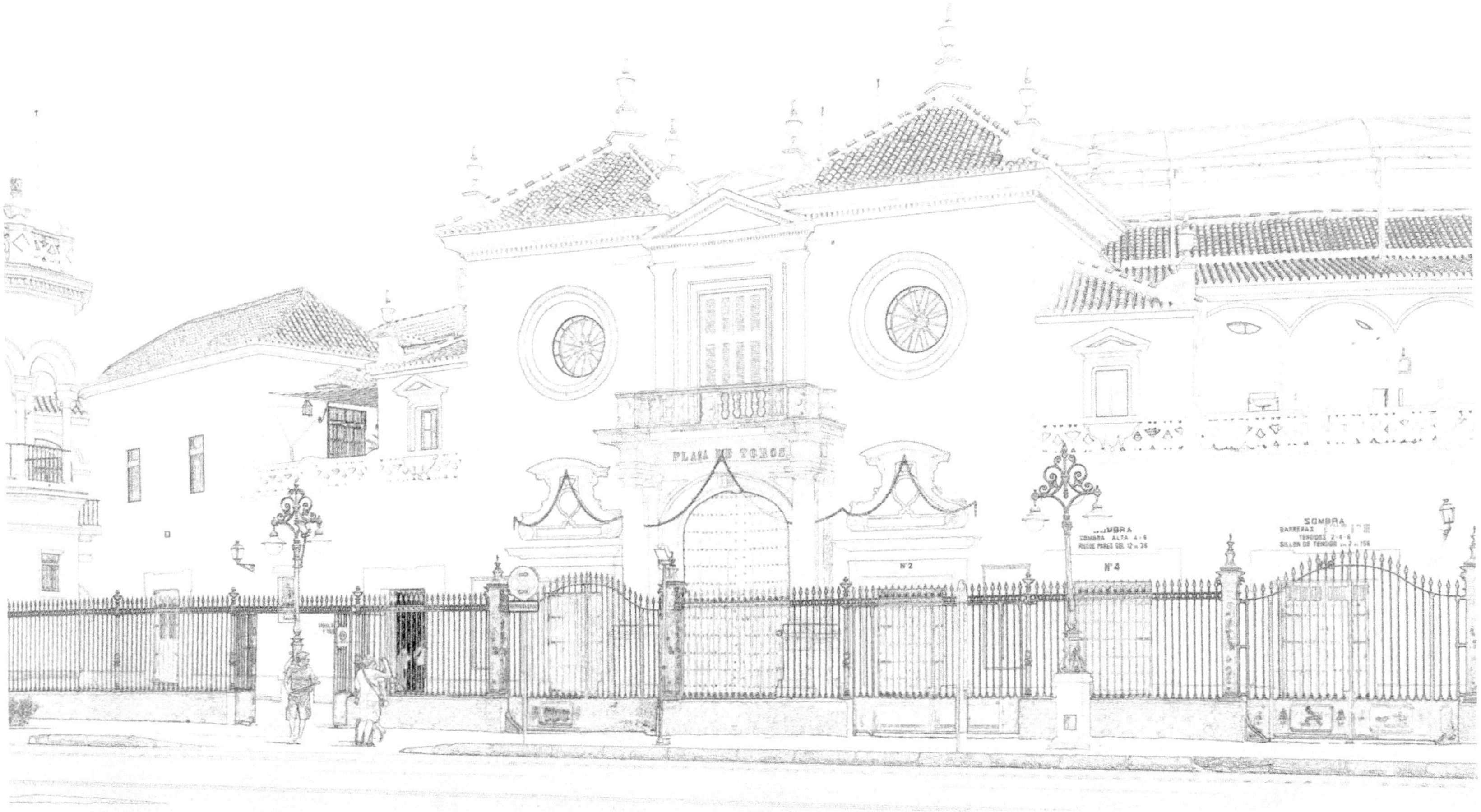
Nº 2
Nº 4
SOMBRA

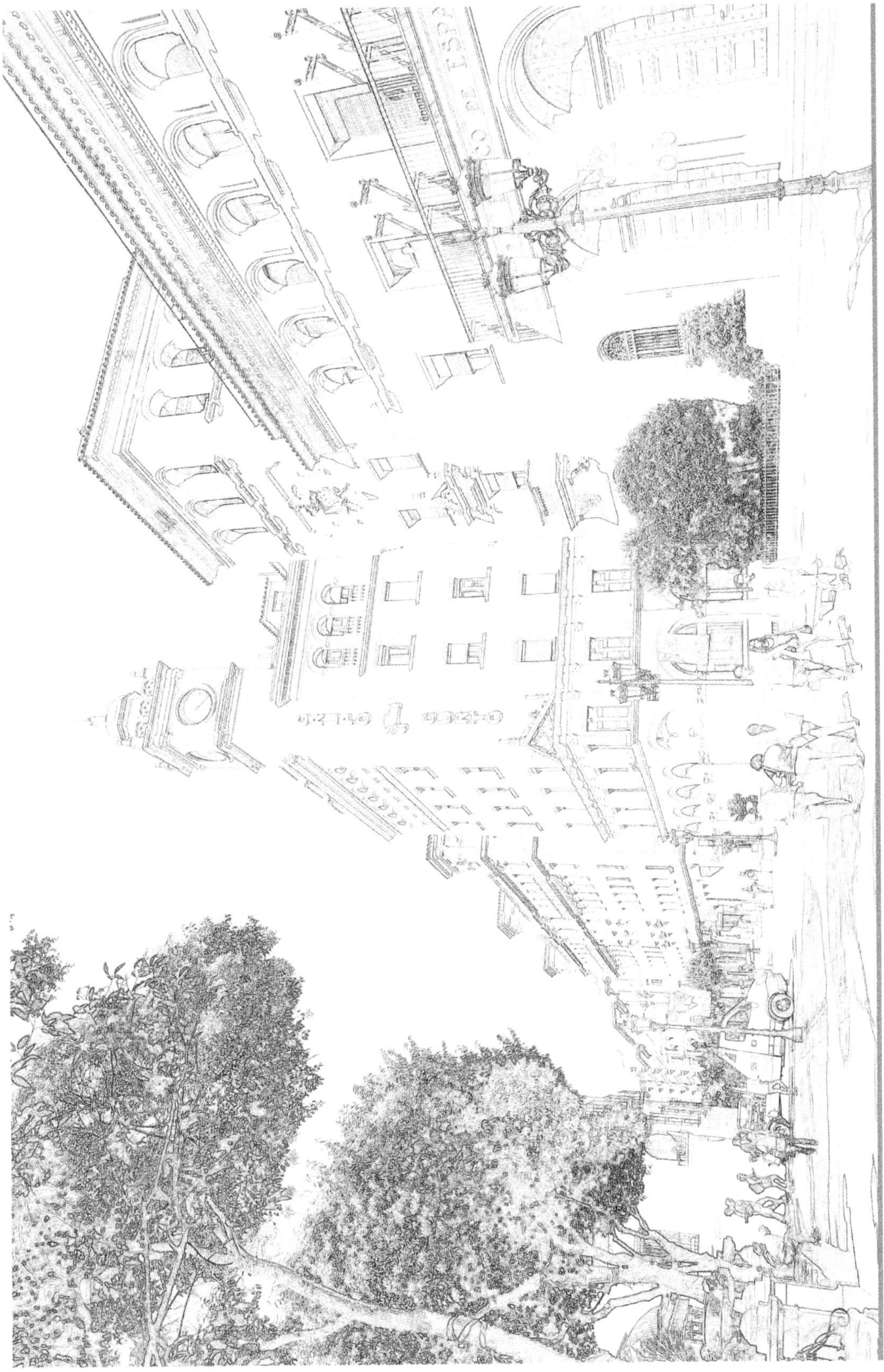

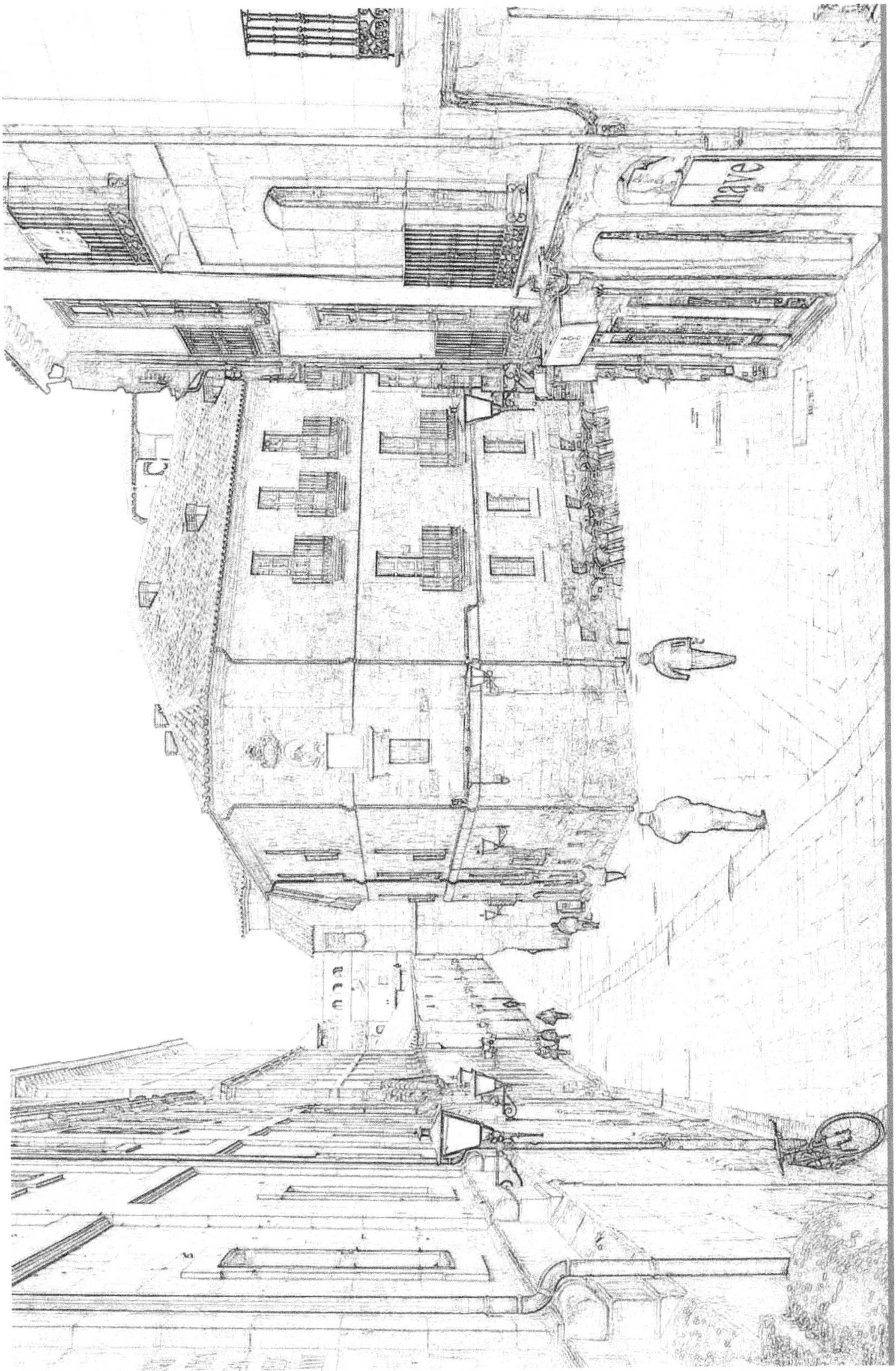

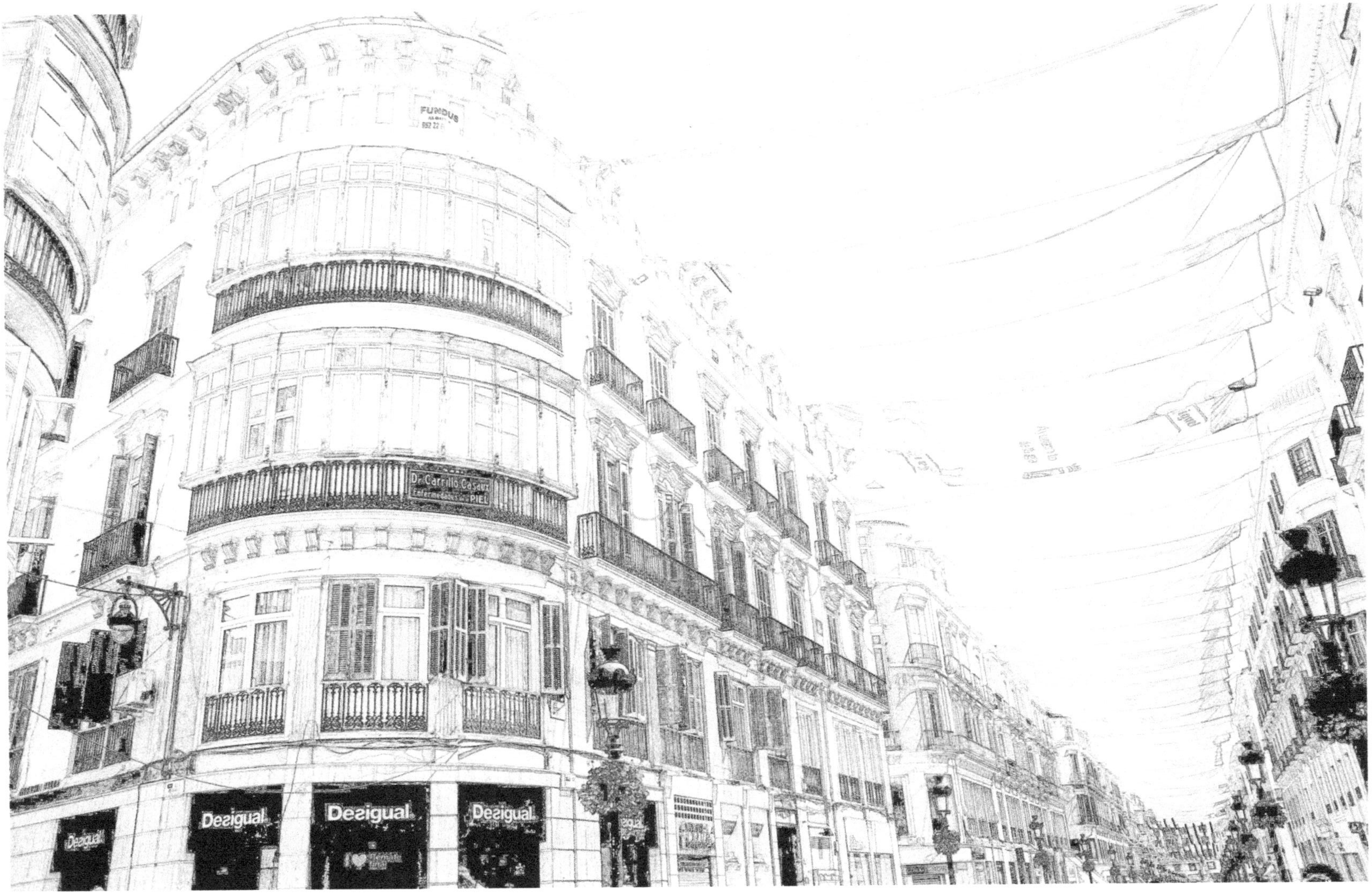
FUNDUS
Desigual
Desigual
Desigual
Desigual

PELUQUERIA SEÑORAS
GAES
Grupo Nexo Canarias
ASESORES INMOBILIARIOS
CONSTRUCCIONES
Y
REFORMAS
922 29307
www.nexocanarias.com

Thank you

PDF Version this book :
http://bit.ly/sketch_7

Don't Miss Another our Books.

I enjoyed designing this book.
It is a compliation of swear words with another stress release coloring designs: Flowers, Mandala, Zentangle etc.
It introduces you to a new coloring experience.
I hope you will enjoy them.
After a hard day, you just need to relax.

Sit down and color the things you can't say.
Enjoy Now !

ISBN : 1535184353

Made in the USA
Columbia, SC
26 October 2023